C0-BJG-337

They Played Baseball for the Dodgers?

A History of Forgotten Players from Brooklyn to Los Angeles

By Jeff Wagner

COPYRIGHT

Dedication

This book is dedicated to the memory of my father, Jim Wagner, who took me to my first professional basketball game in 1966, my first professional hockey game in 1969, my first professional baseball game in 1971, and my first professional football game in 1975. He not only introduced me to the world of sports, but instilled the importance of good sportsmanship and team work whenever playing one.

Also to the memory of my sister Julie Martinez, who was probably a bigger local sports fan than I was!

I would like to thank Eric for his extra pair of eyes.

And last but not least, I would also like to thank my loving wife Amy for her support, even though she has little to no interest in baseball. Thanks for the encouragement!

Table of Contents

Introduction

The Dodgers have had an important and storied role in the history of Major League Baseball. Going back to its Brooklyn roots as the Atlantics in 1884, the "Boys in Blue" are one of the most successful franchises in Major League Baseball history, accumulating 11,017 wins (as of 2020), second only to the Giants with 11,194 and one better than the Chicago Cubs. Their .528 winning percentage is also third in baseball history. And their 3.53 team ERA is the best all-time.

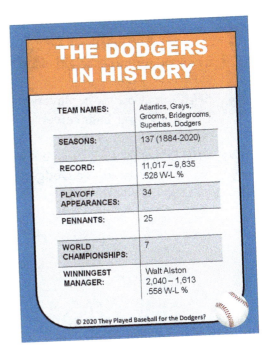

THE DODGERS IN HISTORY

TEAM NAMES:	Atlantics, Grays, Grooms, Bridegrooms, Superbas, Dodgers
SEASONS:	137 (1884-2020)
RECORD:	11,017 – 9,835 .528 W-L %
PLAYOFF APPEARANCES:	34
PENNANTS:	25
WORLD CHAMPIONSHIPS:	7
WINNINGEST MANAGER:	Walt Alston 2,040 – 1,613 .558 W-L %

© 2020 They Played Baseball for the Dodgers?

Everyone knows of the greats who have had legendary careers with the Dodgers: Hall of Famers like Jackie Robinson, Sandy Koufax, Duke Snider, Roy Campanella and Don Drysdale; as well as contemporaries like Mike Piazza and Pedro Martinez, to name just a few.

But did you know that at one time or another, twenty other Hall of Famers have made stops at Ebbets Field or Dodger stadium? As well as a popular country-western television actor, a United States Senator, and five members of the 500 home run club? So I hope you'll enjoy discovering the interesting stories surrounding how and why these, and over thirty-five other players you may have forgotten about or maybe even didn't know, spent time in a Dodger's uniform, and what they did while they were wearing it.

You'll find player stories broken up alphabetically into three categories based on their time with the Dodgers:

- *"The Start of Something Big"*: players who began their career as a Dodger but excelled elsewhere.

- *"Hello and Goodbye"*: players who had short tenures as a Dodger during their career.

- *"The End of the Line"*: players who flourished with other teams but retired as a Dodger.

The Start of Something Big

After observing the nine players that make up this category, players who started their careers as a Dodger, you'll notice one other thing that several have in common: they excelled once they left.

So although these players were all rookies with the Dodgers, they weren't around long enough, or didn't do much when they were there, for many people to remember.

- Casey Stengel
- Chuck Connors
- Dick Williams
- Don Zimmer
- Ernie Lombardi
- Frank Howard
- Gene Mauch
- Paul Konerko
- Pedro Martinez

Casey Stengel

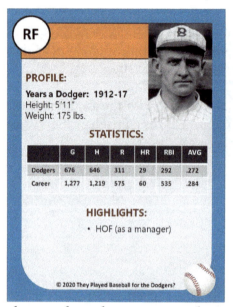

© 2020 They Played Baseball for the Dodgers?

RF

PROFILE:

Years a Dodger: 1912-17
Height: 5'11"
Weight: 175 lbs.

STATISTICS:

	G	H	R	HR	RBI	AVG
Dodgers	676	646	311	29	292	.272
Career	1,277	1,219	575	60	535	.284

HIGHLIGHTS:

• HOF (as a manager)

Charles Dillon "Casey" Stengel is best known for winning 10 American League pennants and seven World Series Championships over a 12 year period as manager of the New York Yankees. But many people don't realize that Stengel had a 15 year career as player for five teams, the first being the Brooklyn Dodgers.

The day after going 4-for-4 in his debut for Brooklyn on September 17, 1912 against Pittsburgh, Stengel joined a player-only poker game as they waited out a rain delay. After finally winning a hand, one of his teammates reportedly commented, "About time you took a pot, Kansas City." The other players caught on, and began calling Stengel "K.C." After one week in the big leagues, Stengel had a nickname, a .478 batting average, and nine RBIs. Casey ended the season with a .316 batting average after playing in 17 games. He finished his career with a .284 batting average, .272 in six years with Brooklyn, and had the distinction of hitting a home run off of Grover Cleveland Alexander in 1916.

Stengel also began his managerial career in Brooklyn, replacing a fired Max Carey in 1933. In three seasons with the Dodgers, Stengel posted a 208-251 record, with their best finish being 5th in 1935. Stengel was let go after the 1936 season. It wouldn't be until 1949 when he would experience success as a manager, where he would lead the Yankees to an impressive 1,149-696 record over a 12 year period. He would end his career as the first manager of the New York Mets from 1962 to 1965.

Chuck Connors

Best known for his role as Lucas McCain on the popular television series "The Rifleman" (1958-63), Chuck Connors is actually one of only 13 athletes in the history of American professional sports to have played both Major League Baseball and professional basketball in the National Basketball Association (NBA).

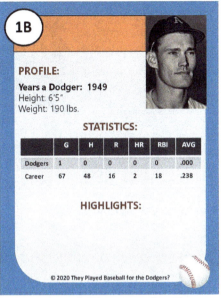

1B

PROFILE:

Years a Dodger: 1949
Height: 6'5"
Weight: 190 lbs.

STATISTICS:

	G	H	R	HR	RBI	AVG
Dodgers	1	0	0	0	0	.000
Career	67	48	16	2	18	.238

HIGHLIGHTS:

© 2020 They Played Baseball for the Dodgers?

Following a military discharge in 1946, the 6' 6" Connors joined the newly formed Boston Celtics of the NBA. He played 53 games for Boston, averaging 4.5 points a game, before leaving the team early in the 1947–48 season.

Connors attended spring training in 1948 with the Brooklyn Dodgers but did not make the squad. He played two seasons for the Dodgers' AAA team before playing one game with Brooklyn in 1949, where he hit into a double play in his only at-bat. After two more seasons in the minors, the Dodgers traded Connors to the Chicago Cubs on October 10, 1950. In 1951, Connors played in 66 games for the Cubbies, hitting .239 with two home runs and 18 RBIs.

After being sent down to the minors again, Connors decided to call it a career after getting a casting call for the Spencer Tracy/Katherine Hepburn movie, "Pat and Mike". Upon getting the five minute part as a police captain, Connors decided to pursue acting full-time.

Dick Williams

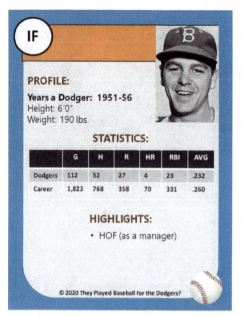

PROFILE:

Years a Dodger: **1951-56**
Height: 6'0"
Weight: 190 lbs.

STATISTICS:

	G	H	R	HR	RBI	AVG
Dodgers	112	52	27	4	23	.232
Career	1,823	768	358	70	331	.260

HIGHLIGHTS:

• HOF (as a manager)

© 2020 They Played Baseball for the Dodgers?

Dick Williams was the quintessential utility man, playing 13 seasons in Major League Baseball with five different teams, while playing six different positions. His first five seasons were with Brooklyn, where he played in 112 games and hit .232 with four home runs. Williams went on to hit .260 with 70 home runs in a career which saw him play in 1,823 games.

William's managerial resume, however, was quite different.

As a rookie manager in 1967, he inherited a Boston Red Sox team that had finished ninth in the ten-team American League in both of the previous two seasons. He and his coaches improved the Sox by 20 wins that year, and took them to the 1967 World Series.

In William's first year with the Oakland A's in 1971, the team won the American League Western Division championship for the first time since moving to Oakland, then won the 1972 and 1973 World Series. In 1979-80, he helped turn around the Montréal Expos by leading them to consecutive 90+ win seasons for the first time in the history of the franchise, while guiding them to second place finishes in the National League Eastern Division both years. And in 1984, Williams took what had been a perennial losing San Diego Padres team to their first World Series after a 13-year history with only one season at or above .500.

In all, Williams was only the second manager in baseball history to win pennants for three different teams (Boston, Oakland and San Diego).

Don Zimmer

While playing for the Dodgers AAA St. Paul team in 1953, Zimmer was hit on the side of the head by a pitch, fracturing his skull and leaving him unconscious for 10 days. Because blood clots were forming on his brain, he was given spinal taps every two or three days. Eventually three holes were drilled into the right side of his head to relieve pressure.

IF

PROFILE:
Years a Dodger: 1954-59, 63
Height: 5'9"
Weight: 165 lbs.

STATISTICS:

	G	H	R	HR	RBI	AVG
Dodgers	459	303	145	43	161	.228
Career	1,095	773	353	91	352	.

HIGHLIGHTS:
• 1x All-Star

© 2020 They Played Baseball for the Dodgers?

You wouldn't think a person who went through all of that would step onto a baseball field again. But in 1955, that's what Don Zimmer did. As Pee Wee Reese's backup, Zimmer played in 88 games for Brooklyn, batting .239 while collecting 15 home runs and 50 RBIs. In the post season, Zimmer started the first two games of the World Series at second base and played in games six and seven enroute to helping the Dodgers win the 1955 World Series.

Zimmer stuck around with the Dodgers after they moved to Los Angeles, and played in a total of 437 games with them between 1954 and 1959 (and 22 games during a brief stint in 1963). In 1960, Zimmer was traded to the Cubs, where he played two seasons before finishing his career with the New York Mets, Cincinnati Reds and the Washington Senators. With the Cubs, Zimmer made his one and only All-Star team in 1961.

Upon retirement, Zimmer began a second career as a coach and manager that lasted 43 years, beginning in 1971 with the San Diego Padres and ending in 2014 with the Tampa Bay Rays. During that time, he would amass an 885-858 record as manager of the San Diego Padres (1972-73), Boston Red Sox (1976-80), Texas Rangers (1981-82) and Chicago Cubs (1988-1991).

Ernie Lombardi

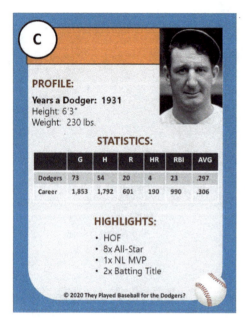

PROFILE:

Years a Dodger: 1931
Height: 6'3"
Weight: 230 lbs.

STATISTICS:

	G	H	R	HR	RBI	AVG
Dodgers	73	54	20	4	23	.297
Career	1,853	1,792	601	190	990	.306

HIGHLIGHTS:

- HOF
- 8x All-Star
- 1x NL MVP
- 2x Batting Title

© 2020 They Played Baseball for the Dodgers?

On January 19, 1931, Brooklyn purchased the contract of Ernesto Natali Lombardi for $50,000 and two players from the minor league Oakland Oaks of the Pacific Coast League. Brooklyn skipper Wilbert Robinson, however, favored seasoned veterans over rookies, which left Lombardi on the bench behind Al Lopez. When given the opportunity, Lombardi produced, hitting .275 in 43 starts at catcher.

Lombardi's stay in Brooklyn was short, however, and on March 14, 1932, he was part of a six-player deal that sent him to the Cincinnati Reds, where he went on to play nine seasons.

Lombardi played in five All-Star games as a Red, and won the batting title and league MVP in 1938. Four years later, the 34-year old backstop surprised everyone by hitting .330 and winning his second National League batting title in five years, this time as a Boston Brave. No light achievement, as it would be 64 years before another catcher would capture a batting crown, when Joe Mauer of the Minnesota Twins did it in 2006. It would be 70 years before another National League catcher won the batting title when Buster Posey of the San Francisco Giants captured the title in 2012.

Lombardi was posthumously inducted into the National Baseball Hall of Fame in 1986.

Frank Howard

An All-American in basketball at Ohio State University, Frank Howard was drafted by the Philadelphia Warriors of the NBA. He instead signed with the Dodgers organization, and after a handful of appearances in 1958 and 1959 succeeded Carl Furillo as Los Angeles' right fielder in 1960.

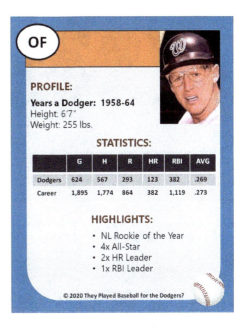

PROFILE:

Years a Dodger: 1958-64
Height: 6'7"
Weight: 255 lbs.

STATISTICS:

	G	H	R	HR	RBI	AVG
Dodgers	624	567	293	123	382	.269
Career	1,895	1,774	864	382	1,119	.273

HIGHLIGHTS:

- NL Rookie of the Year
- 4x All-Star
- 2x HR Leader
- 1x RBI Leader

© 2020 They Played Baseball for the Dodgers?

Howard was named the National League's Rookie of the Year in 1960 after batting .268 with 23 home runs and 77 RBI. He belted 98 homers in the following four seasons, most prominently in a 1962 campaign in which he batted .296 with 31 home runs and finished among the National League's top five players in RBI (119) and slugging (.560).

By 1963, however, Howard's production began to drop, in part to the team's 1962 move into pitcher-friendly Dodger Stadium which hurt power hitters. As a result, speedier outfielders like Willie Davis were seen as more in line with the club's future. After batting .226 in 1964, the 27 year-old power hitter was traded to the Washington Senators in December 1964 in a seven-player deal which brought future All-Star starter Claude Osteen to Los Angeles.

While in Washington, Howard would lead the National League in home runs twice, smacking out 44 in 1968 and 1970, while playing in four All-Star games.

Gene Mauch

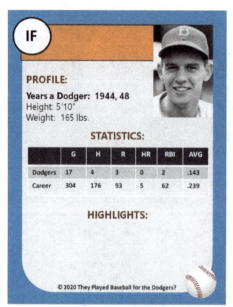

PROFILE:

Years a Dodger: 1944, 48
Height: 5'10"
Weight: 165 lbs.

STATISTICS:

	G	H	R	HR	RBI	AVG
Dodgers	17	4	3	0	2	.143
Career	304	176	93	5	62	.239

HIGHLIGHTS:

© 2020 They Played Baseball for the Dodgers?

Although known in the minor leagues as being a fiery utility infielder, Gene Mauch would never play more than 72 games in any one of his nine major league seasons. Instead, he would make his reputation as a clever, arrogant major league manager who managed the most years (26) and the most games (3,942) of any manager who never won a pennant.

As a player, however, Mauch made his major-league debut for the Dodgers against the Philadelphia Phillies on Opening Day, April 18, 1944. He went 0-for-2 in the 4-1 Dodgers loss at Shibe Park in Philadelphia. Mauch picked up his first career hit the next day, and also had two RBIs in a 5-4 Dodgers win, but he lasted only three more games. After a total of 15 at-bats and with a .133 batting average, Mauch was sent down to the minors.

After serving two years in the military, Brooklyn dealt Mauch and three other players to the Pittsburgh Pirates in early 1947 for Al Gionfriddo and $100,000 cash. Mauch played 16 games as a Pirate, starting seven. That December, the Pirates sent Mauch back to the Dodgers with Billy Cox and Preacher Roe.

Mauch started the 1948 season again wearing Dodger blue, playing in 12 games and starting three. He batted just .154 before being placed on waivers for good on June 7.

In 1960, Mauch began a 26 year managerial career which saw him skipper the Philadelphia Phillies, Montreal Expos, Minnesota Twins and California Angels. He would finish with a 1,902-2037 record.

Paul Konerko

Prior to being drafted by the Dodgers with the 13th pick in the first round of the 1994 MLB draft, Paul Konerko had been on the radar of Dodgers management since he was 13 years old where he played catcher for Scottsdale Chaparral High School in Arizona. As a senior, Konerko hit .564 with 12 homers and 50 RBIs to help deliver the first state baseball title for Chaparral.

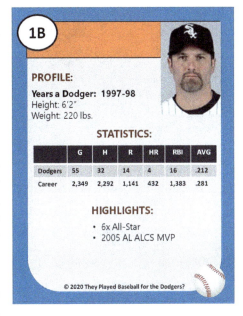

PROFILE:

Years a Dodger: 1997-98
Height: 6'2"
Weight: 220 lbs.

STATISTICS:

	G	H	R	HR	RBI	AVG
Dodgers	55	32	14	4	16	.212
Career	2,349	2,292	1,141	432	1,383	.281

HIGHLIGHTS:

- 6x All-Star
- 2005 AL ALCS MVP

© 2020 They Played Baseball for the Dodgers?

He is one of four Dodgers position players to have been twice selected for the Dodgers organization's "Minor League Player of the Year" award, along with Billy Ashley, Joc Pederson, and Gavin Lux.

Konerko was converted to an outfielder/first baseman and played parts of the 1997 and 1998 seasons with the Dodgers, hitting just four home runs in 151 at bats. On July 4, 1998, Konerko was traded with lefty pitcher Dennys Reyes to the Cincinnati Reds for All-Star closer Jeff Shaw. Konerko played 26 games with the Reds before being shipped to the Chicago White Sox, where he would play the next 16 years.

During his time in Chicago, Konerko would blast 432 home runs, drive in 1,383 runs and hit .281. He would be an All-Star six times, and help the 2005 White Sox win their first World Series since 1917.

Pedro Martinez

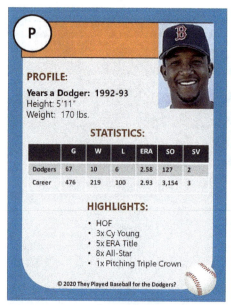

PROFILE:

Years a Dodger: 1992-93
Height: 5'11"
Weight: 170 lbs.

STATISTICS:

	G	W	L	ERA	SO	SV
Dodgers	67	10	6	2.58	127	2
Career	476	219	100	2.93	3,154	3

HIGHLIGHTS:

- HOF
- 3x Cy Young
- 5x ERA Title
- 8x All-Star
- 1x Pitching Triple Crown

© 2020 They Played Baseball for the Dodgers?

Pedro Martinez was originally signed by the Dodgers as an amateur free agent in 1988. After pitching in the Dodgers farm system for over three years, he made his major league debut on September 24, 1992 for the Dodgers against the Cincinnati Reds, working two scoreless innings of relief. He made his first start for the Dodgers on September 30, losing to the Reds 3-1.

Martinez turned in a strong 1993 season as the Dodgers' setup man, going 10–5 with a 2.61 ERA and 119 strikeouts in 65 games. His 107 innings led all National League relievers. With the Dodgers in need of a second baseman after a contract dispute with Jody Reed, Martinez was traded to the Montreal Expos for Delino DeShields before the 1994 season.

It was during a bullpen session in Montreal that manager Felipe Alou encouraged Martinez to modify his primary grip on the fastball from two-seam to four-seam. The transformation was dramatic. His fastball, already one of the quickest in the league, was now being thrown with near-perfect control and a break that would frequently fool hitters.

After four seasons in Montreal, including a final season where he posted a 17-6 record and 1.90 ERA, Martinez left the cash-strapped Expos for greener pastures in Boston, and signed with the Red Sox as a free agent in 1998. Martinez would go on to win three Cy Young awards and five ERA titles in seven seasons with Boston, and pitch in eight All-Star games overall before retiring in 2009 after brief stops with the New York Mets and Philadelphia Phillies.

Hello and Goodbye

These well-known players were technically Dodgers, but were only around for a handshake and a quick cup of coffee. None began or ended their careers as a Dodger, and some were around for only part of a season. Nevertheless, these 22 big name players will always be members of the Dodger blue family.

- Al Oliver
- Bill Skowron
- Bobby Bonilla
- Dick Allen
- Eric Davis
- Frank Robinson
- Fred McGriff
- Gary Carter
- Gary Sheffield
- Hack Wilson
- Heinie Manush
- Jim Bunning
- Jim Thome
- Joe McGinnity
- Manny Ramirez
- Nomar Garciaparra
- Paul Waner
- Phil Garner
- Rabbit Maranville
- Rocky Colavito
- Tony Lazzeri
- Willie Randolph

Al Oliver

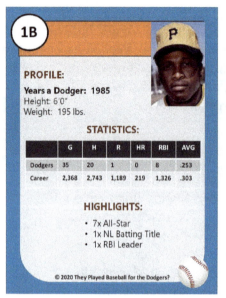

PROFILE:

Years a Dodger: 1985
Height: 6'0"
Weight: 195 lbs.

STATISTICS:

	G	H	R	HR	RBI	AVG
Dodgers	35	20	1	0	8	.253
Career	2,368	2,743	1,189	219	1,326	.303

HIGHLIGHTS:

- 7x All-Star
- 1x NL Batting Title
- 1x RBI Leader

© 2020 They Played Baseball for the Dodgers?

In 1983, 36-year old Al Oliver hit an even .300, drove in 84 runs, and made the All-Star team for the Montreal Expos. In 1984, however, the Expos decided to move in the direction of youth, and started to deal away some of their veteran players. So on February 27, 1984, the Expos peddled Oliver to the San Francisco Giants.

On August 21, 1984 after 91 games with the Giants, Oliver was involved in one of the shortest trades in baseball history, some 500 feet, to the visiting Philadelphia Phillies. After playing 29 games with the Phillies, the Dodgers acquired the 38 year-old Oliver with an eye toward using him in left field, his first real outfield action since 1980.

Oliver's return to regular outfield duty in 1985 did not go well, however, as the veteran made four errors in 17 games, so he served mainly as a pinch-hitter for Los Angeles that season. He played in 35 games total, making 85 plate appearances while hitting .253 and driving in eight runs. Not content with his playing time, Oliver asked to be traded some place where he could be used. The Dodgers obliged, sending him to the Toronto Blue Jays in early July 1985 for Len Matuszek, whom the Phillies had dealt away not long after Oliver. Although the return to the American league with the designated hitter rule gave Oliver more at-bats, he decided to call it a career after the season when he drew no interest in the free agent market in 1986.

In 18 seasons, Oliver hit .303 with 2,743 hits and 1,326 RBIs.

Bill Skowron

Bill "Moose" Skowron signed with the New York Yankees in September 1950 as an amateur free agent and played his first game for the Yankees on April 13, 1954. In nine seasons with the Bronx Bombers, Skowron played in six All-Star games and won five World Series Championships.

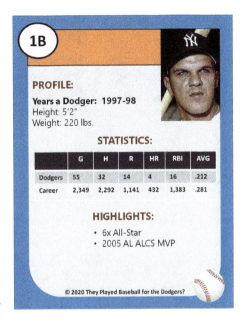

1B

PROFILE:

Years a Dodger: 1997-98
Height: 5'2"
Weight: 220 lbs.

STATISTICS:

	G	H	R	HR	RBI	AVG
Dodgers	55	32	14	4	16	.212
Career	2,349	2,292	1,141	432	1,383	.281

HIGHLIGHTS:

- 6x All-Star
- 2005 AL ALCS MVP

© 2020 They Played Baseball for the Dodgers?

Needing pitching help, and with young and aspiring Joe Pepitone at first base, the Yankees traded Skowron to the Dodgers on November 26, 1962 for Stan Williams, who had won 43 games during the past three seasons. Although Skowron floundered against National League pitching, batting just .203 in 237 at bats with four home runs, he stunned his former team in the 1963 World Series, leading the Dodgers with a .385 average and a home run, as Los Angeles swept New York in four straight games.

Despite expectations of remaining in Los Angeles, Skowron returned to the American League when the Washington Senators purchased him from the Dodgers on December 6, 1963.

Skowron retired after the 1967 season following stops with the Chicago White Sox and California Angels, including his final All-Star appearance in 1965 with Chicago, compiling a career batting average of .282 with 211 home runs and 888 RBIs.

Stan Williams, by the way, spent two seasons with the Yankees, going 10-13 with a 3.43 ERA in 31 starts.

Bobby Bonilla

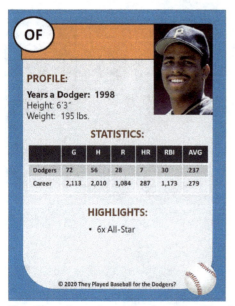

PROFILE:

Years a Dodger: 1998
Height: 6'3"
Weight: 195 lbs.

STATISTICS:

	G	H	R	HR	RBI	AVG
Dodgers	72	56	28	7	30	.237
Career	2,113	2,010	1,084	287	1,173	.279

HIGHLIGHTS:

• 6x All-Star

© 2020 They Played Baseball for the Dodgers?

In his first six seasons with the Pittsburgh Pirates, Bobby Bonilla was an All-Star four times, averaging .284 for the club he began his career with.

In 1992, he left the Bucs and signed a lucrative 5-year, $29 million contract with the New York Mets. More on that contract later.

Following three mediocre seasons in New York, and two better ones in Baltimore after the Mets traded him there, Bonilla signed with the Florida Marlins as a free agent. Upon helping them win the 1997 World Series. Marlins owner Wayne Huizenga disassembled his team, as he sold, failed to re-sign, or traded most of the key players. As a result, Bonilla was traded, along with Gary Sheffield and three others, to the Dodgers for Mike Piazza and Todd Zeile, who were then flipped as well. After batting .237 in 72 games with the Dodgers, Bonilla was bounced back to the Mets for Mel Rojas after the 1998 season.

Now back to that 1992 free-agent contract. In 1999, prior to being released by the Mets, Bonilla agreed to have the remainder of his contract bought out and accepted deferred payments that would begin 12 years later in 2011 and continue until 2035. So on July 1 of each year, Bonilla receives a check for $1,193,248.20 from the Mets on what the media refers to as "Bobby Bonilla Day." Bonilla, in case you're wondering, retired after the 2001 season.

Dick Allen

As a child, Dick Allen spent hours batting around stones while listening to the Brooklyn Dodgers' and his favorite player, Jackie Robinson.

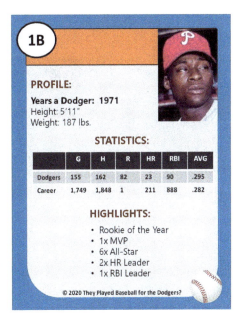

PROFILE:

Years a Dodger: 1971
Height: 5'11"
Weight: 187 lbs.

STATISTICS:

	G	H	R	HR	RBI	AVG
Dodgers	155	162	82	23	90	.295
Career	1,749	1,848	1	211	888	.282

HIGHLIGHTS:
- Rookie of the Year
- 1x MVP
- 6x All-Star
- 2x HR Leader
- 1x RBI Leader

© 2020 They Played Baseball for the Dodgers?

Some dozen years later with the Philadelphia Phillies, Allen would have a rookie season widely regarded as being among the greatest ever. In 1964, Allen led the league in runs (125), triples (13), extra base hits (80), and total bases (352); and finished in the top five in batting average (.318), hits (201), and doubles (38).

Prior to the 1970 season, the Phillies traded Allen to the St. Louis Cardinals for Curt Flood, who then refused to report to the Phillies as part of the trade and then notoriously sued baseball in an unsuccessful attempt to overthrow the reserve clause and be declared a free agent. Coincidentally, the player the Phillies received as compensation for Flood not reporting, Willie Montañez, hit 30 home runs as a rookie in 1971 to eclipse Allen's Phillies rookie home run record of 29, set in 1964.

Allen's boyhood dreams would come true on October 5, 1970 when, in need of a 2nd baseman, the Cardinals traded him to the Dodgers for former rookie-of-the-year second baseman Ted Sizemore and catcher Bob Stinson.

Allen would have a good year at the plate in 1971 for the Dodgers, hitting .295 with 23 home runs and 90 RBIs in 155 games. On December 2, 1971, however, he was traded to the Chicago White Sox for pitcher Tommy John and infielder Steve Huntz.

Eric Davis

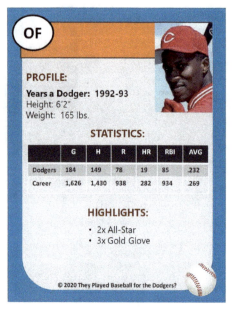

PROFILE:

Years a Dodger: 1992-93
Height: 6'2"
Weight: 165 lbs.

STATISTICS:

	G	H	R	HR	RBI	AVG
Dodgers	184	149	78	19	85	.232
Career	1,626	1,430	938	282	934	.269

HIGHLIGHTS:

- 2x All-Star
- 3x Gold Glove

© 2020 They Played Baseball for the Dodgers?

Most baseball fans are aware of what Eric Davis did as a Cincinnati Red: great defense, two-time All-Star, first player to hit 30 home runs and steal 50 bases, and World Series champion in 1990. But what Davis did in the latter part of his career is what was truly amazing and inspirational.

Beginning with a lacerated kidney suffered during game 4 of the 1990 World Series, injuries would start to sabotage Davis' play, and in 1991 he was traded to the Los Angeles Dodgers for Tim Belcher and John Wetteland. Davis suffered several more injuries in 1992 and was largely ineffective with the Dodgers, playing in 184 games over two seasons while hitting .232 overall. On August 23, 1993, the Dodgers dealt Davis to the Detroit Tigers for a player to be named later, who a week later would be pitcher John DeSilva.

After sitting out 1995 with injuries, Davis returned with a strong 1996 outing during his second stint with the Reds before signing with the Baltimore Orioles in 1997. Davis started 1997 well before being set back by a stomach ailment that would later be diagnosed as colon cancer. After having a portion of his colon removed and following a series of chemotherapy treatments, Davis remarkably rejoined the Orioles in time for the playoffs, and even hit a game winning home run in the American League Championship series against Cleveland. The Orioles brought Davis back in 1998 where he had one of his best years in his career, playing in 131 games, hitting .327 while knocking out 28 home runs and driving in 89.

Davis played in parts of three more seasons before retiring in 2001.

Frank Robinson

Fourteen-time All-Star, 586 career home runs, two-time league MVP, one of only 17 players to win the Triple Crown, and National League Rookie of the Year. Toss in batting .300 nine times, hitting 30 home runs eleven times, and being the first black manager in Major League history, as well as a player/manager, and you have one Frank Robinson.

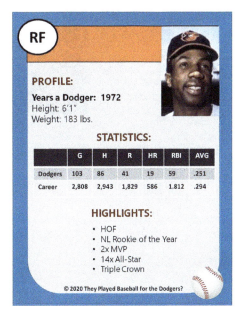

RF

PROFILE:

Years a Dodger: 1972
Height: 6'1"
Weight: 183 lbs.

STATISTICS:

	G	H	R	HR	RBI	AVG
Dodgers	103	86	41	19	59	.251
Career	2,808	2,943	1,829	586	1.812	.294

HIGHLIGHTS:

- HOF
- NL Rookie of the Year
- 2x MVP
- 14x All-Star
- Triple Crown

© 2020 They Played Baseball for the Dodgers?

After leading Baltimore to four pennants in six years, Robinson's tenure with the Orioles came to a surprising end after the 1971 season. With Don Baylor waiting in the wings, the Orioles found Robinson and his $130,000 salary expendable. The 36-year-old was sent to the Dodgers for Doyle Alexander, Bob O'Brien, Sergio Robles and Royle Stillman. Robinson played 103 games for Los Angeles in 1972, compiling a .251 batting average, 59 RBIs, 86 hits, and 19 home runs.

During the 1972 winter meetings,, Robinson was traded along with Bill Singer, Bobby Valentine, Billy Grabarkewitz and Mike Strahler to the California Angels for Andy Messersmith and Ken McMullen. The transaction was the result of Robinson's request for regular playing time, something Dodgers general manager Al Campanis wanted for the team's younger prospects.

On September 12, 1974, the Angels traded Robinson to the Cleveland Indians, who three weeks later named him their manager while persuading him to continue playing. In his first at bat as a player/manager for Cleveland in 1975, Robinson hit a home run off of Doc Medich of the New York Yankees.

Fred McGriff

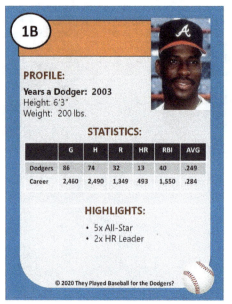

1B

PROFILE:

Years a Dodger: 2003
Height: 6'3"
Weight: 200 lbs.

STATISTICS:

	G	H	R	HR	RBI	AVG
Dodgers	86	74	32	13	40	.249
Career	2,460	2,490	1,349	493	1,550	.284

HIGHLIGHTS:

- 5x All-Star
- 2x HR Leader

© 2020 They Played Baseball for the Dodgers?

After successful stops in Toronto, San Diego and Atlanta, including a World Series title with the Braves in 1995, 34 year-old Tampa native Fred "Crime Dog" McGriff was given the opportunity to play for his hometown team when he was picked up by the expansion Tampa Devil Rays on November 18, 1997.

After three seasons with the Rays, where he averaged 29 home runs and 104 RBIs, Tampa sent McGriff to the Cubs to hit behind Sammy Sosa. After a fifth place finish in 2002, the Cubs let McGriff walk, and on New Years Eve 2002, the Dodgers signed the slugger with the hope of inserting a steady power bat in the middle of their lineup. And perhaps attract some fans who wanted to see him break the 500-homer mark, as McGriff was only 22 dingers away.

Injuries, however, would end that hope, as McGriff missed extended periods with knee, hip, and groin injuries. He played in 86 games for the Dodgers in 2003, and ended up with 13 homers and 41 RBIs while only batting .249. Although the Dodgers did not re-sign McGriff for 2004, his old team in Tampa did.

But after hitting .181 average and belting only two home runs in his sporadic play through mid-July, the Devil Rays released the 40 year-old McGriff on July 28, 2004, seven home runs shy of 500. McGriff officially announced his retirement during spring training 2005 when he received no interest from other teams. McGriff and Gary Sheffield are the only players ever to hit at least 30 home runs in one season for five different teams.

Gary Carter

In 1977, 23-year-old Gary "Kid" Carter's Hall-of-Fame career took off. Hitting .284 with 31 home runs and 84 RBIs, Carter began giving fellow National League catcher Johnny Bench something he'd yet experience as a pro: serious competition for starting catcher in the All-Star game. Carter went on to play in 10 straight All-Star games from 1979-1988, supplanting Bench for good when the long time Red retired in 1983.

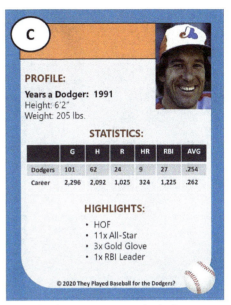

PROFILE:

Years a Dodger: 1991
Height: 6'2"
Weight: 205 lbs.

STATISTICS:

	G	H	R	HR	RBI	AVG
Dodgers	101	62	24	9	27	.254
Career	2,296	2,092	1,025	324	1,225	.262

HIGHLIGHTS:

- HOF
- 11x All-Star
- 3x Gold Glove
- 1x RBI Leader

© 2020 They Played Baseball for the Dodgers?

Following a stellar career in Montreal, the Expos traded Carter to the Mets following the 1984 season after turning down Carter's salary demands. "Kid" went on to have three strong seasons with the Mets and picked up his only World Series ring in 1986. By 1988, injuries began to plague the 34-year-old, and after only playing in 50 games in 1989, the Mets cut ties with their aging catcher.

After signing with the San Francisco Giants in early 1990, Carter played in 92 games, clubbing out nine home runs, driving in 27, and hitting .254 while platooning with Terry Kennedy,

After the Giants released him on November 5, 1990, Carter signed with the team he had followed as a boy — the Dodgers — after a non-roster invitation from manager Tommy Lasorda. Carter began the season backing up Mike Scioscia, but when Scioscia was sidelined by a broken hand, Carter played every game for two straight weeks, including both ends of a doubleheader against the Braves. In 101 games with the Dodgers, Carter hit .254 with nine homers and 27 RBIs. Carter did not file for free agency after the 1991 season, and the Dodgers placed him on waivers.

Gary Sheffield

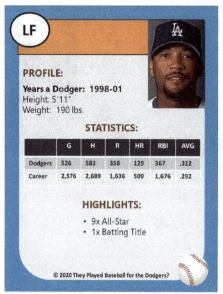

PROFILE:

Years a Dodger: 1998-01
Height: 5'11"
Weight: 190 lbs.

STATISTICS:

	G	H	R	HR	RBI	AVG
Dodgers	526	583	358	129	367	.312
Career	2,576	2,689	1,636	509	1,676	.292

HIGHLIGHTS:

- 9x All-Star
- 1x Batting Title

© 2020 They Played Baseball for the Dodgers?

When Gary Sheffield was eleven years old, he was selected to the Belmont Heights Little League All-Star team, which included future Chicago Cubs #1 pick Ty Griffin and future Major Leaguer Derek Bell. The team made it to the finals of the 1980 Little League World Series with 20-3 and 16-0 victories over Rhode Island and Washington, but lost to Taiwan 4-3. Sheffield, a pitcher at that time, hit .600 for the series.

In his 22-year major league career as a third baseman and outfielder, Gary Sheffield blasted 509 home runs, drove in 1,676 runs, and posted an impressive .292 batting average for a power hitter. Also eye-catching is the fact that Sheffield played for eight different teams.

On May 14, 1998, he was traded along with Manuel Barrios, Charles Johnson, Bobby Bonilla, and Jim Eisenreich by the Miami Marlins to his fourth team, the Dodgers, for Mike Piazza and Todd Zeile.

Sheffield finished the season with the Dodgers batting .316 and hitting 16 homers while driving in 57 runs. In 3½ seasons with Los Angeles, he hit 129 home runs and drove in 367 runs while making three All-Star teams. But after the 2001 season, he began lobbying for a trade after voicing his unhappiness with the team's direction.

As a result, Sheffield was traded to the Atlanta Braves in January 2002 for Brian Jordan, Odalis Pérez, and Andrew Brown. After two seasons with the Braves, he became a free agent for the first time in his long career on October 27, 2003, and would sign with the New York Yankees two months later.

Hack Wilson

On August 8, 1925, one of the most lob-sided trades in baseball history took place. After starting his career with three lackluster seasons as a New York Giant, the Giants dealt Lewis Robert "Hack" Wilson, a husky 5'6", 190 lb, 25-year-old outfielder to the Chicago Cubs for right fielder Earl Webb. Webb played in four games for the Giants in 1925 and went hitless in three at bats.

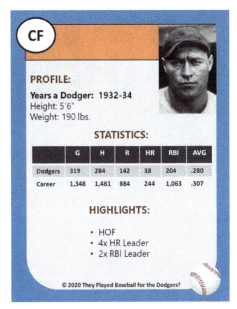

CF

PROFILE:

Years a Dodger: 1932-34
Height: 5'6"
Weight: 190 lbs.

STATISTICS:

	G	H	R	HR	RBI	AVG
Dodgers	319	284	142	38	204	.280
Career	1,348	1,461	884	244	1,063	.307

HIGHLIGHTS:

- HOF
- 4x HR Leader
- 2x RBI Leader

© 2020 They Played Baseball for the Dodgers?

Wilson, on the other hand, spent the next six seasons with the Cubs, hitting .322 with 190 home runs and 769 RBIs. He led the National League in homers in his first season in Chicago, as well as in 1927, 1928 and 1930. In 1930, Wilson had a season for the record books when he knocked out 56 home runs, a still all-time record 191 RBIs, and a .356 batting average.

In December 1931, the Cubs traded Wilson to the St. Louis Cardinals, and less than a month later, the Cardinals sent him to Brooklyn for minor league outfielder Bob Parham and $25,000. Wilson hit .297 with 23 home runs and 123 RBIs for Brooklyn in 1932. Early in the 1933 season, Wilson hit a ninth-inning game-winning pinch-hit inside-the-park grand slam home run at Ebbets Field—the first pinch-hit grand slam in Dodger history, and only the third inside-the-park pinch-hit grand slam in major league history. By season's end his offensive totals had dropped substantially, and he was hitting .262 when the Dodgers released him mid-way through the 1934 season.

Heinie Manush

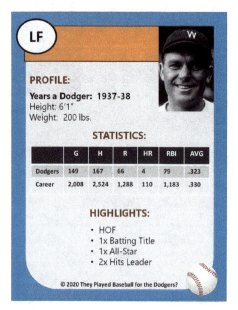

PROFILE:

Years a Dodger: 1937-38
Height: 6'1"
Weight: 200 lbs.

STATISTICS:

	G	H	R	HR	RBI	AVG
Dodgers	149	167	66	4	79	.323
Career	2,008	2,524	1,288	110	1,183	.330

HIGHLIGHTS:

- HOF
- 1x Batting Title
- 1x All-Star
- 2x Hits Leader

© 2020 They Played Baseball for the Dodgers?

During the first 11 years of his 17 year career, which began in 1923, Henry Emmett "Heinie" Manush posted batting averages that included .362, .355, .350, .349, .342, .334, and .378 twice. Amazingly, he only won the league's batting title once during that time.

Nicknamed "Heinie" as a result of his German ancestry, Manush signed with the Dodgers as a free agent in December, 1936 after being released by the Boston Red Sox following a two year batting slump which saw his average "dip" to .273 in 1935 and .291 in 1936.

In spring training with the Dodgers, Manush broke out of his batting slump, leading the Florida circuit with a .571 average. He became the Dodgers' starting right fielder in 1937, and in his first season facing National League pitching, Manush compiled a .333 batting average, ninth highest in the league. Manush began the 1938 season with the Dodgers, but his batting slump returned as his average fell to .238 through 17 games and was released soon after.

The 36-year old Manush would sign with the Pittsburgh Pirates late in 1938 as insurance for their pennant drive, serving primarily as a pinch hitter. After starting the 1939 with the Pirates, Manush was released on June 7, 1939 after 12 at bats and subsequently retired.

In the 1934 All-Star Game, Manush drew a walk off of Carl Hubbell prior to Hubbell's historical striking out of Babe Ruth, Lou Gehrig, Jimmie Foxx, Al Simmons and Joe Cronin in succession. Manush finished his Hall-of-Fame 2,008-game career with a .330 batting average, 2,524 hits, 1,288 runs scored and 1,183 RBIs.

Jim Bunning

Can you name the only person to be voted into the Major League Baseball Hall-of-Fame, serve in the United States House of Representatives and United States Senate? If you couldn't, you can now! That would be Jim Bunning. And in 1964 with the Philadelphia Phillies, Bunning would throw the first perfect game by a National League pitcher since 1880.

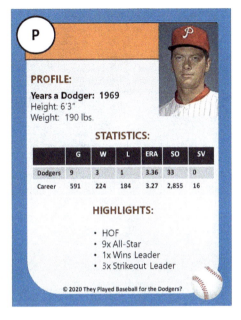

P

PROFILE:

Years a Dodger: 1969
Height: 6'3"
Weight: 190 lbs.

STATISTICS:

	G	W	L	ERA	SO	SV
Dodgers	9	3	1	3.36	33	0
Career	591	224	184	3.27	2,855	16

HIGHLIGHTS:

- HOF
- 9x All-Star
- 1x Wins Leader
- 3x Strikeout Leader

© 2020 They Played Baseball for the Dodgers?

Bunning's perfect game was also the first no-hitter by a Phillies pitcher since Johnny Lush no-hit Brooklyn in 1906. He is one of only seven pitchers to have thrown both a perfect game and an additional no-hitter, and one of five players to have thrown a no-hitter in both leagues. Bunning was also the first pitcher to pitch a no-hitter, win 100 games, and record 1,000 strikeouts in both leagues.

Bunning pitched for Philadelphia through 1967, when the Phillies began to rebuild. As a result, the Phillies traded him to the Pittsburgh Pirates before the 1968 season, and played with them until being traded to the Dodgers in August 1969. With the Dodgers, Bunning pitched in nine games, going 3-1 with a 3.36 ERA before being released on October 22, 1969.

After resigning with Philadelphia, Bunning pitched for two more seasons before retiring after the 1971 season at the age of 40.

In his post-baseball political career, Bunning served in the United States House of Representatives from 1987 to 1999, and the United States Senate from 1999 through 2011.

Jim Thome

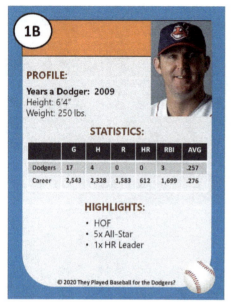

1B

PROFILE:
Years a Dodger: 2009
Height: 6'4"
Weight: 250 lbs.

STATISTICS:

	G	H	R	HR	RBI	AVG
Dodgers	17	4	0	0	3	.257
Career	2,543	2,328	1,583	612	1,699	.276

HIGHLIGHTS:
- HOF
- 5x All-Star
- 1x HR Leader

© 2020 They Played Baseball for the Dodgers?

By the time the Chicago White Sox traded Jim Thome to the Dodgers on August 21, 2009, the 38 year-old had already played 18 seasons of Major League baseball and pounded out 541 career home runs.

Thome waived his no-trade clause to join the Dodgers with the hopes of winning his first World Series title. The Dodgers were on the verge of winning the National League West pennant, and subsequently won the the National League division series over the St. Louis Cardinals before losing to his old team, the Philadelphia Phillies, in the National League Championship Series.

Thome's only appearances with the Dodgers were as a pinch hitter, due to chronic foot injuries that limited his mobility on the field. He hit .235 with no home runs and three RBIs in 17 at-bats with the Dodgers. After the season, Thome filed for free agency, eventually signing with the Minnesota Twins.

In his career, the Hall-of-Famer's 612 home runs ranks eighth in baseball history. He is also the fourth major leaguer to hit 100 home runs for three different teams. The slugger also drove in 1,699 RBIs, while hitting a respectable .276 during his 22 years in Major League Baseball. Despite the number of home runs hit, however, Thome only led the league in round trippers once with 47 in 2003 as a Phillie. Thome's season high was the year before when he pounded 52 homers with the Cleveland Indians, finishing second to Alex Rodiguez's 57.

Joe McGinnity

A strong case could be made that Joe McGinnity had the greatest rookie season of any pitcher in Major League Baseball history. Just take a look at these numbers from his 1899 season with the Baltimore Orioles: 48 games started, a 28-16 record, and a 2.68 ERA. Almost just amazing is that he did so by only striking out 74 batters in 366 innings, or less than two strikeouts per nine innings. His top pitch, a rising curve ball thrown underhand style that he nicknamed "Old Sal", was the primary reason why.

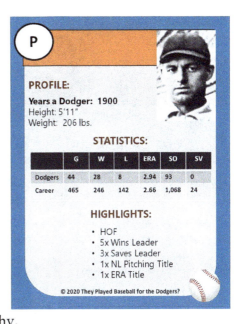

PROFILE:

Years a Dodger: 1900
Height: 5'11"
Weight: 206 lbs.

STATISTICS:

	G	W	L	ERA	SO	SV
Dodgers	44	28	8	2.94	93	0
Career	465	246	142	2.66	1,068	24

HIGHLIGHTS:

- HOF
- 5x Wins Leader
- 3x Saves Leader
- 1x NL Pitching Title
- 1x ERA Title

© 2020 They Played Baseball for the Dodgers?

Prior to the 1900 season, the National League condensed from 12 teams to eight. Baltimore and Brooklyn, which had the same owners, were merged into one team. So, McGinnity suddenly found himself pitching for the Brooklyn Superbas (later the Dodgers), and went on to post a 28-8 record that season. With the formation of the American League and a new Baltimore Orioles team, McGinnity turned down a more lucrative offer from Brooklyn to return to Baltimore in 1901.

Appropriately nicknamed "Iron Man", McGinnity worked 3,441 innings and won 246 games in just 10 years, including two amazing seasons in 1903 and 1904 when he won a total of 66 games. In 1903, McGinnity was involved in 51 decisions, winning 31 and losing 20. During August in 1903, he pitched and won both ends of a doubleheader three times; a feat he accomplished twice more in his career. In 1904, McGinnity had one of the greatest seasons of any pitcher when he went 35-8 in 51 starts while posting a microscopic 1.61 ERA. "Iron Man" started 92 games and pitched 842 innings in those two seasons alone.

Manny Ramirez

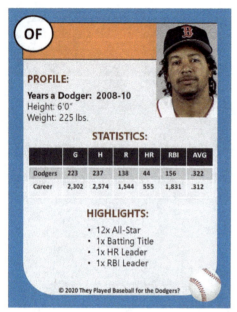

PROFILE:

Years a Dodger: 2008-10
Height: 6'0"
Weight: 225 lbs.

STATISTICS:

	G	H	R	HR	RBI	AVG
Dodgers	223	237	138	44	156	.322
Career	2,302	2,574	1,544	555	1,831	.312

HIGHLIGHTS:

- 12x All-Star
- 1x Batting Title
- 1x HR Leader
- 1x RBI Leader

© 2020 They Played Baseball for the Dodgers?

After spending 16 years with the Cleveland Indians and Boston Red Sox where he was a 12-time All-Star, led the American League with 165 RBIs in 1999, a .349 batting average in 2002, and 43 home runs in 2004, 36 year-old Manny Ramirez was traded to the Dodgers on July 31, 2008 in a three team trade involving Boston and the Pittsburgh Pirates.

In the 53 games he played in after the trade, Ramirez drove in 53 runs and hit .396. The Dodgers won the National League Division Series in 2008 but lost the National League Championship series in five games. In both series, Ramirez hit .516 with four home runs and nine RBIs.

In 2009, however, the bat of the now 37 year-old Ramirez began to cool off a bit, but he still hit a respectable .290 in 104 games while clouting 19 home runs and driving in 63 runs. Ramirez tested positive for a banned substance early that season, however, and was suspended for 50 games from May 7 through July 2.

In 2010, Ramirez got off to a good start with the Dodgers, batting .322 through the end of June. But after three stints on the disable list, he managed to only play in two games in July and five in August. As a result, the Dodgers placed Ramirez on waivers, where he was selected by the Chicago White Sox on August 30.

For his career, Ramirez hit 555 home runs (15th all-time), drove in 1,831 runs (19th all-time) and posted a particularly impressive .312 lifetime batting average over 19 seasons.

Nomar Garciaparra

In 2000, Anthony Nomar Garciaparra had the highest single-season batting average by a right-handed hitter in the post-war era, batting .372, and in 1999 and 2000 was the first right-handed batter to win the American League batting title in consecutive seasons since Joe DiMaggio.

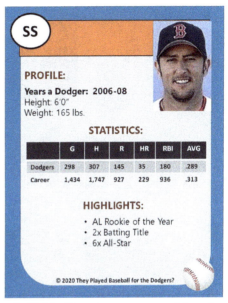

PROFILE:

Years a Dodger: 2006-08
Height: 6'0"
Weight: 165 lbs.

STATISTICS:

	G	H	R	HR	RBI	AVG
Dodgers	298	307	145	35	180	.289
Career	1,434	1,747	927	229	936	.313

HIGHLIGHTS:

- AL Rookie of the Year
- 2x Batting Title
- 6x All-Star

© 2020 They Played Baseball for the Dodgers?

In 2001, however, Garciaparra suffered a wrist injury, the first in a series of significant injuries that plagued the remainder of his career. After playing in 156 games in 2002 and 2003, Garciaparra would only break the 100 game mark twice in the next eight years. So after 8 ½ years and two batting titles in Boston, the popular shortstop was traded to the Chicago Cubs in July 2004, just three months before the Red Sox would win their first World Series in 86 years.

After a year-and-a-half with the Cubs, Garciappara signed as a free agent with the Dodgers, his hometown team, for the 2006 season. Healthy for the first time since 2003, he had his best season in three years, finishing with a .303 average, 20 home runs and 93 RBIs while playing in 122 games, the most since 2003 as well. Hitting .358 at the All-Star break, he was selected to his first National League All-Star team, but this time at a new position — first base — where he would finish with just four errors the entire season. His lofty batting average declined to .303 by the end of the season, however, as nagging injuries returned. By 2008, Garciappara's playing time had dwindled to 55 games, and his average followed at .264. As a result, the Dodgers didn't re-sign the 34 year-old after the season ended, and he finished his career with one season with the Oakland A's where he played in 65 games and hit .281.

Paul Waner

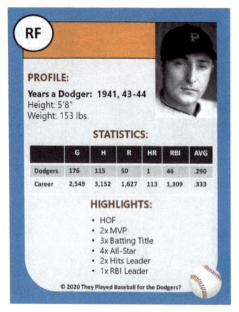

RF

PROFILE:
Years a Dodger: 1941, 43-44
Height: 5'8"
Weight: 153 lbs.

STATISTICS:

	G	H	R	HR	RBI	AVG
Dodgers	176	115	50	1	46	.290
Career	2,549	3,152	1,627	113	1,309	.333

HIGHLIGHTS:
- HOF
- 2x MVP
- 3x Batting Title
- 4x All-Star
- 2x Hits Leader
- 1x RBI Leader

© 2020 They Played Baseball for the Dodgers?

Paul "Big Poison" Waner played for four teams during a 20 year career between 1926 and 1945, most notably his first 15 seasons with the Pittsburgh Pirates. During that time, he led the National League in batting three times and was voted the National League's MVP in 1927.

Waner was the seventh player to accumulate over 3,000 hits in a career, collected 200 or more hits in eight different seasons, and had a lifetime batting average of .333. Waner also had one six-hit game, and five five-hit games.

Waner and his younger brother Lloyd hold the record for career hits by brothers with 5,611, outpacing the three Alou brothers (Felipe, Matty, and Jesús), and the three DiMaggio brothers (Joe, Dom, and Vince), who had 5,094 and 4,853 respectively.

After his 15-year stint with the Pirates, Waner played the next four seasons with the Boston Braves and Brooklyn Dodgers. He made two stops in Brooklyn actually, one in 1941 which lasted all of 11 games before he was released after hitting .171. Waner joined the Boston Braves for the remainder of the 1941 season and all of 1942, before re-signing with the Dodgers on January 21, 1943.

Used sparingly the next two seasons in Brooklyn, Waner still hit .311 to go with 35 walks in 82 games in 1943. In 1944, the 41 year-old was mainly used as a pinch hitter, and hit .287 with 39 hits in 138 at bats. Waner was released on September 1 that year and picked up by the Yankees where he went 1 for 7. After one pinch hit appearance for the Yankees in 1945, Waner retired.

Phil Garner

Originally a third baseman when drafted by the Oakland A's in 1971, Phil Garner was converted to second base as All-Star Sal Bando occupied the position. Garner won two World Series with Oakland in 1973 and 1974, mostly as a bench player. His breakout season was in 1976 when he collected eight home runs and 74 RBI's while being named to his first All Star team.

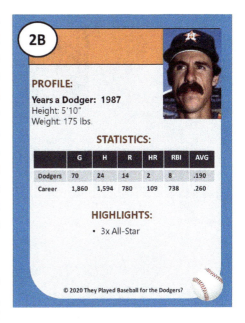

2B

PROFILE:

Years a Dodger: 1987
Height: 5'10"
Weight: 175 lbs.

STATISTICS:

	G	H	R	HR	RBI	AVG
Dodgers	70	24	14	2	8	.190
Career	1,860	1,594	780	109	738	.260

HIGHLIGHTS:

• 3x All-Star

© 2020 They Played Baseball for the Dodgers?

Nicknamed "Scrap-Iron" due to his gritty style of play, Garner's best year was in 1977 when he hit 17 HR's, had 77 RBI's, stole 32 bases, and scored 99 runs as a Pittsburgh Pirate after being traded to the steel city prior to the start of the season. Two years later in 1979, he was a member of the World Series champion Pirates, batting .417 in the 1979 National League Championship Series and .500 (12 for 24) in the World Series. After All-Star seasons in 1980 and 1981, Garner was traded to the Houston Astros, where he spent the next 5 ½ years.

Garner's career wound down in 1987 and 1988, as the 38-year old was traded from the Houston to the Dodgers on June 19, 1987 in exchange for a player to be named later, who a week later became minor league pitcher Jeff Edwards. Garner was a part-time player for Los Angeles, hitting .206 for the season with five home runs and 23 RBIs in 70 games. He played his last game October 2, 1988 for the San Francisco Giants, and got a base on balls as a pinch-hitter.

Garner would go on to win 985 games managing the Milwaukee Brewers, Detroit Tigers and the Astros between 1992 and 2007.

Rabbit Maranville

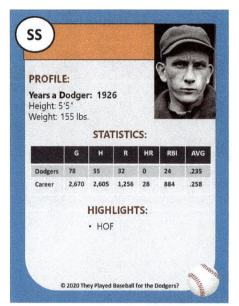

PROFILE:

Years a Dodger: 1926
Height: 5'5"
Weight: 155 lbs.

STATISTICS:

	G	H	R	HR	RBI	AVG
Dodgers	78	55	32	0	24	.235
Career	2,670	2,605	1,256	28	884	.258

HIGHLIGHTS:

- HOF

© 2020 They Played Baseball for the Dodgers?

Standing only 5'5", 21 year-old Walter "Rabbit" Maranville finished third in the 1913 MVP voting during his first full season with the Boston Braves, even though he hit just .247 with two home runs in 143 games. The following year, as the Braves cleanup hitter, Maranville was the runner-up in the MVP voting to teammate Johnny Evers despite batting just .246 and hitting four home runs. Both sound inconceivable, but this was the time of the dead ball era, a period between 1900 and 1919 when the league leader in home runs had fewer than 10 in 13 of those seasons. Runs during that time were primarily generated using stolen bases and the hit-and-run.

After eight years in Boston, Maranville was dealt to the Pittsburgh Pirates in January, 1921 where he played four years before the Pirates sent him to the Chicago Cubs to become their player/manager in 1925. After being released by the Cubs at season's end, "Rabbit" was claimed by Brooklyn on November 9, 1925. In 78 games during 1926, the 34 year-old Maranville hit .235 with no home runs and 24 RBIs. He was released by Brooklyn on August 21, 1926.

Known as much for his zany antics and funny stories as for anything he accomplished on the field, Rabbit Maranville compiled a lifetime batting average of just .258, never hit higher than .284, and had no more than five home runs or 78 RBIs in a single season. Instead, it was his outstanding glove work that kept him in the big leagues for 23 seasons and eventually earned him a plaque in Cooperstown.

Rocky Colavito

Although Rocco "Rocky" Colavito Jr. was born in the Bronx, his hometown Yankees had no interest in his baseball services as a youth. But the Cleveland Indians did. Prior to joining the Indians in 1956, Colavito showed off his arm by throwing a baseball from home plate over the center-field fence some 436 feet away during a minor league game.

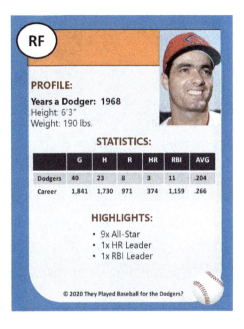

RF

PROFILE:

Years a Dodger: 1968
Height: 6'3"
Weight: 190 lbs.

STATISTICS:

	G	H	R	HR	RBI	AVG
Dodgers	40	23	8	3	11	.204
Career	1,841	1,730	971	374	1,159	.266

HIGHLIGHTS:

- 9x All-Star
- 1x HR Leader
- 1x RBI Leader

© 2020 They Played Baseball for the Dodgers?

During the next 11 seasons, Colavito would become the first Indian ever to have back-to-back 40 home runs seasons, become the second player in American League history to hit four consecutive home runs in a nine inning game, win home run and RBI titles, and play on nine All-Star teams.

In March 1968, after spending the prior season in Cleveland and Chicago, he was purchased by the Dodgers from the White Sox. Colavito hit three home runs for the Dodgers in his inaugural National League season, and batted .204 with 23 hits in 60 games. He was released by the Dodgers on July 11 that season.

Four days later, Colavito got his chance to play for the Yankees, as the team signed him on July 15. On August 25, the 35 year-old Colavito became the last position player until Brent Mayne in 2000 to be credited as the winning pitcher in a game. He pitched 2 2/3 scoreless innings as a reliever in the first game of a doubleheader against the league-leading Tigers. He also tamed the Tigers by scoring the winning run for the Yankees in the eighth inning, and hitting a home run in the second game. Colavito had 20 hits including five home runs in 39 games before being released by the Yankees on September 30, 1968, and shortly after retired as a player.

Tony Lazzeri

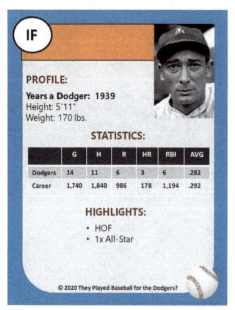

PROFILE:

Years a Dodger: 1939
Height: 5'11"
Weight: 170 lbs.

STATISTICS:

	G	H	R	HR	RBI	AVG
Dodgers	14	11	6	3	6	.282
Career	1,740	1,840	986	178	1,194	.292

HIGHLIGHTS:

- HOF
- 1x All-Star

© 2020 They Played Baseball for the Dodgers?

When most people think of the New Yankees of the 1920's and 1930's, the names Babe Ruth, Lou Gehrig, Joe DiMaggio, and Bill Dickey come to mind. You rarely hear the name Tony Lazzeri mentioned. But this Hall-of-Fame infielder played a big role in the success of those Yankee teams, starting with his rookie season in 1926 when he hit knocked out 18 home runs and drove in 117.

On May 24, 1936, Lazzeri had a game for the record books when he hit two grand slam home runs, the first player to ever do that, and drove in 11 runs, which is still an American League record. Lazzeri is also one of only 14 Major Leaguers to hit for the natural cycle (single, double, triple, home run in order) and the only player to complete the natural cycle with a grand slam.

After the 1937 season, the Yankees released Lazzeri after hitting .244 in 126 games. The 33-year-old infielder then signed with the Chicago Cubs as a player-coach in 1938. The Cubs released him after losing to his old team, the Yankees, in a World Series in which Lazzeri would go 0 for 2.

Lazzeri went on to sign with the Brooklyn Dodgers prior to the 1939 season, but was released on May 13 after batting .282 in 14 games with them. The next day, the New York Giants signed him to play third base where he went on to play 13 games for the Giant before being released on June 7, 1939. Lazzeri soon retired as a player at the age of 35, ending his 14-year career which saw him win five World Series championships. Sadly, Lazzeri would die seven years later of a heart attack at the age of 42.

Willie Randolph

After 13 years with the New York Yankees, Willie Randolph was granted free agency following the 1988 season. During his tenure in pinstripes, he ranked among the team's all-time leaders in games played (1,694), runs (1,027), hits (1,731) and stolen bases (251).

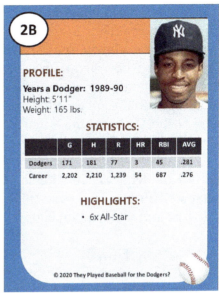

2B

PROFILE:

Years a Dodger: 1989-90
Height: 5'11"
Weight: 165 lbs.

STATISTICS:

	G	H	R	HR	RBI	AVG
Dodgers	171	181	77	3	45	.281
Career	2,202	2,210	1,239	54	687	.276

HIGHLIGHTS:
• 6x All-Star

© 2020 They Played Baseball for the Dodgers?

On December 10, 1988, 34 year-old Randolph signed with the Dodgers and in 1989 led the team in batting average (.282) and hits (155), while making the National League All-Star team. His 145 games played that season were his highest since playing in 153 in 1979.

In 1990, he appeared in 26 games for the Dodgers before being traded to the Oakland A's for outfielder Stan Javier on May 13. Before joining the A's, Randolph hit .271 in 26 games. Randolph hit .257 in 93 games with the A's, helping them reach the 1990 World Series against the Cincinnati Reds.

In 1991, Randolph signed with the Milwaukee Brewers and hit .327 with 54 RBIs in 124 games. The following year, at the age of 37, Randolph returned to New York, but with the cross-rival Mets, and hit .252 in 90 games before retiring after the 1992 season.

The End of the Line

Throughout baseball history, it would not be unusual for a team fighting for a playoff spot to bring on a player in the twilight of their career who was hungry for one final championship run. The hope was that their experience and motivation to win one final time would give the team an added edge during a pennant drive. In the case of the Dodgers, this seemed to happen a lot in the 1990's and early 2000's. And more often than not, the move worked!

So the following are 10 notable players who, although ending their careers with the Dodgers, enjoyed their most productive, glory-filled, or at least memorable years with other teams.

- Boog Powell
- Eddie Murray
- Freddie Lindstrom
- Greg Maddox
- Hoyt Wilhelm
- Jerry Grote
- Juan Marichal
- Leo Durocher
- Mark Belanger
- Rickey Henderson

Boog Powell

In his 14 years as a Baltimore Oriole, John Wesley Powell, nicknamed "Boog" by his dad for being a "mischief bugger" as a kid, hit 30 or more home runs three times, over 20 eight times, and drove in over 100 runs three times. In 1970, he was voted the American League Most Valuable Player when he had 35 homers, 114 RBIs and hit .297.

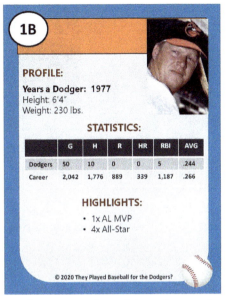

PROFILE:

Years a Dodger: 1977
Height: 6'4"
Weight: 230 lbs.

STATISTICS:

	G	H	R	HR	RBI	AVG
Dodgers	50	10	0	0	5	.244
Career	2,042	1,776	889	339	1,187	.266

HIGHLIGHTS:

- 1x AL MVP
- 4x All-Star

© 2020 They Played Baseball for the Dodgers?

In 1973 and 1974, Powell became a platoon player for the Orioles, and when Baltimore acquired slugging first baseman Lee May from the Houston Astros, Powell became expendable. In 1975, friend and former teammate Frank Robinson joined the Cleveland Indians as their manager, and wanted Powell on his team. So in February 1975, Powell was traded to the Indians for catcher Dave Duncan.

In 1975 a rejuvenated Powell, once again a full-time player, had his best year since 1972 when he blasted 27 home runs, drove in 86 and hit .297. Powell's 1976 season, however, was hampered by a torn thigh muscle. For the first time in his major-league career, he played in fewer than 100 games, only 89 of them at first base, and hit just .209 with nine home runs.

Powell was released at the end of spring training in 1977, and signed with the Los Angeles Dodgers as insurance behind starter Steve Garvey. But after only 53 plate appearances, primarily as a pinch hitter, and hitting just .222, Powell was released on August 31, 1977. At the age of 35, he called it a career.

Eddie Murray

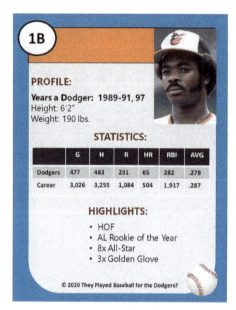

1B

PROFILE:

Years a Dodger: 1989-91, 97
Height: 6'2"
Weight: 190 lbs.

STATISTICS:

	G	H	R	HR	RBI	AVG
Dodgers	477	483	231	65	282	.278
Career	3,026	3,255	1,084	504	1,917	.287

HIGHLIGHTS:

• HOF
• AL Rookie of the Year
• 8x All-Star
• 3x Golden Glove

© 2020 They Played Baseball for the Dodgers?

In 12 years with the Baltimore Orioles, including a Rookie-of-the-Year winning 1977 season where he hit 27 home runs, drove in 88 and batted .283, Eddie Murray was a seven time All-Star. During those years, Murray hit over 25 home runs each season but two, and drove in over 100 runs and hit over .300 five times.

After the Orioles dropped to a 54-107 last place finish in 1988, and with Murray failing to drive in 100 runs for the second consecutive season while seeing his average drop 20 points from two years earlier, the Orioles decided to trade the first baseman rather than pay him his league leading salary. As a result, the Birds sent Murray to the Dodgers for Juan Bell, Brian Holton, and Ken Howell on December 4, 1988.

In his first season with Los Angeles, he hit for a career low .247 with 88 RBIs, 20 home runs, 29 doubles and 147 hits in 160 games. The following year, Murray improved to a .330 average while collecting 95 RBIs, 26 home runs, 22 doubles and 184 hits in 155 games. The 1991 season was his last with the Dodgers, where he hit .260 with 96 RBIs and 19 home runs in 153 games and was named to his final All-Star team. On October 29, 1991, the 35 year-old Murray was granted free agency after the Dodgers wouldn't offer him more than a one-year contract.

In 1987, Murray became the first switch-hitter ever to homer from both sides of the plate in consecutive games. Murray is still in the top 15 all-time in games played (6th - 3,026), RBIs (11th – 1,917), and hits (13th - 3,255), and is 27th in home runs with 504.

Freddie Lindstrom

From 1926 through 1931 Freddie Lindstrom hit .300 or better every year for the New York Giants. In 1928 he led the league with 231 hits and matched that two years later to become only the second player in National League history to have two seasons with more than 230 hits.

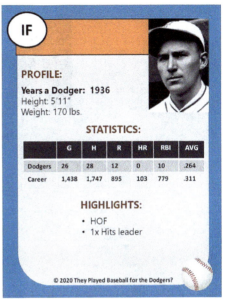

IF

PROFILE:

Years a Dodger: 1936
Height: 5'11"
Weight: 170 lbs.

STATISTICS:

	G	H	R	HR	RBI	AVG
Dodgers	26	28	12	0	10	.264
Career	1,438	1,747	895	103	779	.311

HIGHLIGHTS:
- HOF
- 1x Hits leader

© 2020 They Played Baseball for the Dodgers?

In 1930 Lindstrom became the first third baseman in the twentieth century to hit 20 home runs in a season. He also hit a personal high .379 that year, but amazingly fell 22 points behind the league leader, teammate Bill Terry and his record .401 average.

In 1931, with rumors that legendary John McGraw would soon retire, Lindstrom's name began to surface as a possible replacement. After McGraw stepped down in 1932, Giants ownership instead hired teammate Bill Terry. Angry over being passed over, the Giants would trade Lindstrom to the Pittsburgh Pirates in a three team trade.

After two unproductive seasons in Pittsburgh and one with the Chicago Cubs, Lindstrom was signed as a free agent by the Dodgers in 1936. After 26 games and a .264 batting with Brooklyn, Lindstrom asked for and received his release soon after colliding with infielder Jimmy Jordan while going for a routine pop fly. He played his last major league game on May 15, 1936, at the age of 30.

In 13 big league seasons, Lindstrom hit .300 or better seven times and recorded six 5-hit games. He hit for the cycle on May 8, 1930.

Greg Maddux

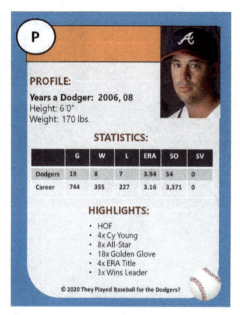

PROFILE:

Years a Dodger: 2006, 08
Height: 6'0"
Weight: 170 lbs.

STATISTICS:

	G	W	L	ERA	SO	SV
Dodgers	19	8	7	3.94	54	0
Career	744	355	227	3.16	3,371	0

HIGHLIGHTS:

- HOF
- 4x Cy Young
- 8x All-Star
- 18x Golden Glove
- 4x ERA Title
- 3x Wins Leader

© 2020 They Played Baseball for the Dodgers?

Prior to joining the Dodgers in 2006, Greg Maddux had already won 300 games, played in eight All-Star games, and won four consecutive Cy Young awards. He also led the league in wins three times, ERA four times, games started eight times, innings pitched five times, and won 17 Gold Glove awards for his fielding.

On July 31, 2006, however, the 40 year-old Maddux was traded for the first time in his career, when the Chicago Cubs sent him to the Dodgers for Cesar Izturis. In his first Dodger start, Maddux threw six no-hit innings before being interrupted by a rain delay. With 15 wins in 2006 (6-3 with the Dodgers), Maddux finished in the league's Top 10 for wins for the 18th time, breaking the record of 17 he had shared with Cy Young and Warren Spahn.

After signing a free-agent contract with the San Diego Padres for 2007, Maddux was traded back to the Dodgers on August 19, 2008. Although only going 2-4 in seven starts with Los Angeles, Maddux did reach two milestones. On September 19, he pitched his 5,000 inning, putting him in 13th place all-time; and on September 27 won his 355th game to pass Roger Clemens and into 8th place all-time. Interesting enough, Maddux did so by only winning 20 games twice in his 23 year career, in 1992 and 1993 (he did win 19 games five times). He is also the oldest pitcher to steal a base, doing so at the age of 42 with the Padres.

A month after pitching four innings of relief during the 2008 post-season for the Dodgers, Maddux announced his retirement.

Hoyt Wilhelm

It's not every day you when you come across a 29-year-old rookie who ended up playing 21 years in the Major Leagues. But that's just what knuckleball specialist Hoyt Wilhelm did. In 1952, Wilhelm, a converted starter who pitched mainly in relief, launched his long career as a member of the New York Giants, where he amazingly won 15 games without starting any of them. He also captured the National League ERA title that year with a 2.43 mark. Two years later, Wilhelm went 12-4 with an ERA of 2.10, again without starting any of the games. In fact, he wouldn't start his first game until 1958 as a member of the Cleveland Indians.

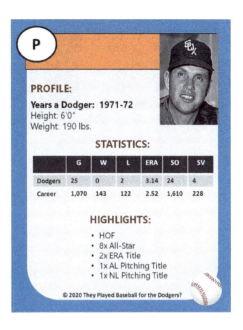

P

PROFILE:

Years a Dodger: 1971-72
Height: 6'0"
Weight: 190 lbs.

STATISTICS:

	G	W	L	ERA	SO	SV
Dodgers	25	0	2	3.14	24	4
Career	1,070	143	122	2.52	1,610	228

HIGHLIGHTS:
- HOF
- 8x All-Star
- 2x ERA Title
- 1x AL Pitching Title
- 1x NL Pitching Title

© 2020 They Played Baseball for the Dodgers?

With the Indians, Wilhelm started six of 30 games in 1958 before being released and claimed by the Baltimore Orioles on August 23rd. Five weeks later, he would no-hit the eventual World Champion New York Yankees 1-0 in only his ninth career start.

Wilhelm signed with the Dodgers as a free agent on July 10, 1971 at the age of 48, and pitched until July 21, 1972 when, just 16 days short of his 50th birthday, was released after appearing in 16 games and posting a 4.62 ERA over 25 innings with the Dodgers. Wilhelm would retire soon after. At the time of his retirement, Wilhelm had pitched in a then major league record 1,070 games, starting 52 of them. He is recognized as the first pitcher to have saved 200 games in his career, and the first pitcher to appear in 1,000 games. He also still holds the Major League record of 124 wins in relief. He would be the first relief pitcher to enter the Hall-of-Fame in 1985.

Jerry Grote

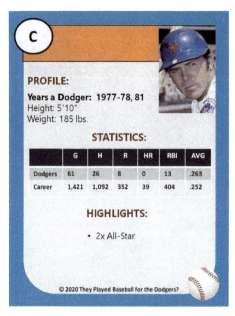

PROFILE:

Years a Dodger: 1977-78, 81
Height: 5'10"
Weight: 185 lbs.

STATISTICS:

	G	H	R	HR	RBI	AVG
Dodgers	61	26	8	0	13	.263
Career	1,421	1,092	352	39	404	.252

HIGHLIGHTS:

• 2x All-Star

© 2020 They Played Baseball for the Dodgers?

Gerald Wayne Grote played the majority of his Major League Baseball career as a catcher for the New York Mets, catching every inning of the franchise's first two World Series appearances: a 1969 win over the Baltimore Orioles and a 1973 loss to the Oakland A's. A two-time All-Star for the National League, Grote is regarded as one of the best defensive catchers of his era.

After 12 years with the Mets, Grote was traded to the Dodgers in October 1977 for two minor leaguers, Daniel Smith and Randy Rogers. Shortly after joining the Dodgers, Grote struck out in his only career at-bat against former battery-mate Tom Seaver, who was now with the Cincinnati Reds.

During his two seasons with the Dodgers, Grote played part-time as a backup to Steve Yeager and appeared in two World Series against the New York Yankees. He retired from professional baseball following the 1978 season after playing in 41 games, only to be lured out in 1981 by the Kansas City Royals, who were short on catchers. On June 3, 1981, at the age of 38, Grote went 3 for 4 with a grand slam home run, a double, and a stolen base, driving in a then team-record seven runs. After the Royals released Grote on September 1, he rejoined the Dodgers a week later, played in one game going 0-for-2, and retired for good after the 1981 season.

Through 2019, Grote ranks among the career leaders for catchers in games played (1,348), putouts (8,081), and fielding percentage (.991). Three decades after his final game as a Met, he had still caught more games than anyone else in club history (1,176).

Juan Marichal

Except for perhaps Sandy Koufax, a strong case could be made that Juan Marichal was the best pitcher of the 1960's. His 191 wins is 27 more than second place Bob Gibson. His 2.57 ERA is bettered only by Koufax's 2.36. He was third in innings pitched and his 45 shutouts led the decade by four over Gibson. In addition, Marichal won 20 games in six seasons over an eight year period that decade, including four in a row. Between 1962 and 1971, the Giants averaged 90 wins a season, while Marichal averaged 20 victories a year.

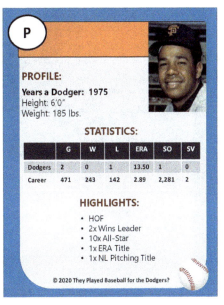

P

PROFILE:

Years a Dodger: 1975
Height: 6'0"
Weight: 185 lbs.

STATISTICS:

	G	W	L	ERA	SO	SV
Dodgers	2	0	1	13.50	1	0
Career	471	243	142	2.89	2,281	2

HIGHLIGHTS:

- HOF
- 2x Wins Leader
- 10x All-Star
- 1x ERA Title
- 1x NL Pitching Title

© 2020 They Played Baseball for the Dodgers?

The 1970's wouldn't be quite as magical for the "Dominican Dandy", however. Following a solid 18-11 campaign in 1971 where he went to his final All-Star game, Marichal posted 6–16 and 11–15 records in 1972 and 1973, after which the Giants sold his contract to the Boston Red Sox on December 8, 1973. Although going 5–1 in 11 starts for Boston, but with a lofty 4.87 ERA, he was released after the season. On March 15, 1975, Marichal signed with the Dodgers, to the displeasure of many Dodger fans who hadn't forgiven Marichal for the infamous "bat" incident with John Roseboro 10 years earlier. It took a personal appeal from Roseboro himself, who by that time was good friends with Marichal, to help calm things down. Marichal's 1975 was short-lived, however, as he gave up nine runs, 11 hits and posted a 13.50 ERA in only two starts before retiring following his last outing on April 16.

Marichal finished his career with 243 victories, 142 losses, 244 complete games, 2,303 strikeouts and a 2.89 ERA over 3,507 innings pitched. He pitched in 10 All-Star games and won one ERA title.

Leo Durocher

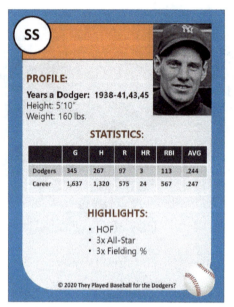

SS

PROFILE:
Years a Dodger: 1938-41,43,45
Height: 5'10"
Weight: 160 lbs.

STATISTICS:

	G	H	R	HR	RBI	AVG
Dodgers	345	267	97	3	113	.244
Career	1,637	1,320	575	24	567	.247

HIGHLIGHTS:
• HOF
• 3x All-Star
• 3x Fielding %

© 2020 They Played Baseball for the Dodgers?

Leo "the Lip" Durocher broke into professional baseball with the minor league Hartford Senators of the Eastern League in 1925. He was called up by the Yankees and played in two games that year. As a starter in 1928, he was nicknamed "The All-American Out" by Babe Ruth. Durocher helped the team win their second consecutive World Series title in 1928, but then, after demanding a raise, was sold to the Cincinnati Reds on February 5, 1930. Durocher spent the remainder of his professional career in the National League where he became a three-time All-Star and fielding percentage leader for shortstops.

On October 4, 1937, Durocher was traded by the St. Louis Cardinals to the Dodgers for four players. Beginning in 1939, Durocher became a player/manager for Brooklyn until 1945 when he retired from playing. During his playing career with the Dodgers, Durocher hit .244 in 345 games. He was an All-Star in 1938 and 1940.

As a manager for the Dodgers, Durocher won 738 games from 1939 through 1946, including 104 in 1942 and 100 in 1941 when his team won the National League pennant. The Dodgers lost the 1941 World Series to the Yankees in five games.

"The Lip" went on to manage until 1973 before retiring with the Houston Astros at the age of 67. During his managerial career, Durocher led his teams to three pennants and one World Series title, while amassing 2,008 wins.

Mark Belanger

Never known for his hitting, supporting just a .228 lifetime average over an 18-year career while holding the American League career record for being pinch-hit for – 333 times –, Mark Belanger's forte was fielding. Winner of eight Golden Glove awards at shortstop, Belanger was so confident in his fielding that he never wore a cup and never dove for a ball.

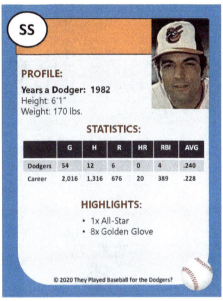

SS

PROFILE:
Years a Dodger: 1982
Height: 6'1"
Weight: 170 lbs.

STATISTICS:

	G	H	R	HR	RBI	AVG
Dodgers	54	12	6	0	4	.240
Career	2,016	1,316	676	20	389	.228

HIGHLIGHTS:
• 1x All-Star
• 8x Golden Glove

© 2020 They Played Baseball for the Dodgers?

Belanger spent 17 of his 18 years with the Baltimore Orioles where he played in five World Series. In 1976, the slick fielding shortstop managed to hit .300 at the All-Star break and was added to the American League's All-Star team for the first and only time. He finished the season with a career high .270 average.

After a falling out with manager Earl Weaver, the 38 year-old Belanger signed with the Dodgers on December 11, 1981 to play one last season. Along with his utility-infielder duties, he handed lineup cards to umpires and pitched batting practice. He walked twice in his final start against flame thrower Nolan Ryan. The last grounder he fielded was from Tony Gwynn on September 21, 1982.

Belanger and Ozzie Smith are the only shortstops to retire with fielding averages over .975 while averaging more than five fielding chances per game.

A skiing accident early in January 1997 led to an unexpected diagnosis of lung cancer that April. Belanger, who began smoking in the 1960's but stopped in 1991, died of the disease on October 6, 1998 at the age of 54.

Rickey Henderson

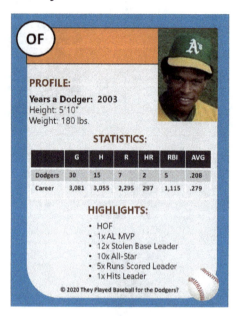

© 2020 They Played Baseball for the Dodgers?

PROFILE:

Years a Dodger: 2003
Height: 5'10"
Weight: 180 lbs.

STATISTICS:

	G	H	R	HR	RBI	AVG
Dodgers	30	15	7	2	5	.208
Career	3,081	3,055	2,295	297	1,115	.279

HIGHLIGHTS:

- HOF
- 1x AL MVP
- 12x Stolen Base Leader
- 10x All-Star
- 5x Runs Scored Leader
- 1x Hits Leader

As the 2003 season began, future Hall-of-Famer Rickey Henderson was without a team for the first time in his 24 year career. He played for the Newark Bears in the independent Atlantic League, hoping for a chance with another major league organization. After being named the Atlantic League All-Star Game MVP, the Dodgers signed the 44 year-old on July 14, 2003 over the All-Star break.

In 30 games with the Dodgers, his ninth and final team, he had 15 hits and three stolen bases, with a .208 batting average. Henderson played his last major league game on September 19, 2003 and was hit by a pitch in his only plate appearance. He would go around and score his 2,295th run, tops in Major League Baseball history.

Henderson wasn't ready to announce his retirement, however, as over the next three years he continued to play minor league ball and accept an occasional Major League invitation as hitting coach, including with the New York Mets in 2006. Henderson did finally concede his "official retirement" on July 13, 2007 at the age of 48.

In addition to ranking first in runs scored with 2,295, Henderson is also the all-time leader in stolen bases (1,406) and leadoff home runs (81), and ranks second all-time in walks (2,190) and is 26th in hits (3,055). For his career, he clouted 297 home runs, drove in 1,115 RBIs, and hit .279. Henderson stole a record 130 bases in 1982, and his 1,406 total is 468 ahead of second place Lou Brock's 938.

Other Players of Note

In the early days of baseball, up into the 1930's, seeing a colorful nickname attached to a player was a pretty common occurrence. For whatever the reason, these catchy nicknames began disappearing in the 1940's and were almost non-existent from the 1950's onward. But here are a few of the most noteworthy who played for the Dodgers early in their history.

- Binky Jones
- Bones Ely
- Boom-Boom Beck
- Boots Poffenberger
- Brickyard Kennedy
- Bunny Fabrique
- Butts Wagner
- Chappie McFarland
- Chink Outen
- Cookie Lavagetto
- Fats Dantonio
- Frenchy Bordagaray
- Goody Rosen
- Happy Smith
- High Pockets Kelly
- Hod Ford
- Hunky Hines
- Jigger Statz
- Judge McCredie
- Kid Carsey
- Lu Blue
- Mysterious Walker
- Pea Ridge Day
- Phenomenal Smith
- Pop Corkhill
- Possum Whitted
- Rowdy Elliott
- Schoolboy Rowe
- Sloppy Thurston
- Snooks Dowd
- Stuffy Stewart
- Sweetbread Bailey
- Welcome Gaston
- Wheezer Dell

The Dodgers by the Numbers

The following shows where the Dodgers franchise ranks among Major League Baseball teams in a variety of categories through the 2020 season, going back to 1884 when baseball in Brooklyn first began.

WINS

Rank	Team	Since	WINS
1	Giants	1883	11,194
2	Dodgers	1884	11,017
3	Cubs	1876	11,016
4	Cardinals	1882	10,948
5	Braves	1876	10,732
6	Reds	1882	10,630
7	Pirates	1882	10,564
8	Yankees	1903	10,411
9	Phillies	1883	9,853
10	Red Sox	1901	9,626

WINNING %

Rank	Team	Since	%
1	Yankees	1903	.570
2	Giants	1883	.535
3	Dodgers	1884	.528
4	Cardinals	1882	.520
5	Red Sox	1901	.518
6	Cubs	1876	.514
7	Indians	1901	.512
8	Reds	1882	.505
9	Tigers	1901	.504
10	Pirates	1882	.503

RUNS

Rank	Team	Since	RUNS
1	Cubs	1876	99,513
2	Giants	1883	97,567
3	Cardinals	1882	97,246
4	Braves	1876	96,065
5	Reds	1882	95,083
6	Pirates	1882	94,463
7	Dodgers	1884	94,224
8	Phillies	1883	93,055
9	Yankees	1903	89,355
10	Red Sox	1901	87,054

ERA

Rank	Team	Since	ERA
1	Dodgers	1884	3.53
2	Giants	1883	3.58
3	Yankees	1903	3.65
4	Braves	1876	3.67
5	Cardinals	1882	3.67
6	Cubs	1876	3.68
7	Pirates	1882	3.73
8	Reds	1882	3.75
9	Wh. Sox	1901	3.78
10	Mets	1962	3.80

WORLD CHAMPIONSHIPS

Rank	Team	Since	WS #
1	Yankees	1903	27
2	Cardinals	1882	11
3	Red Sox	1901	9
4	A's	1901	9
5	Giants	1883	8
6	Dodgers	1884	7
7	Pirates	1882	5
8	Reds	1882	5
9	Tigers	1901	4
10	Braves	1876	3

HALL OF FAMERS

Rank	Team	Since	HOF
1	Giants	1883	57
2	Braves	1876	53
3	Dodgers	1884	50
4	Cardinals	1882	47
5	Yankees	1903	46
6	Cubs	1876	45
7	A's	1901	41
8	Pirates	1882	40
9	Red Sox	1901	37
10	Reds	1882	36

Source: *"Baseball Reference"*: https://www.baseball-reference.com/

The Dodgers – a Timeline

The following outlines some of the milestones of the Dodgers beginning with their 1884 birth as the Brooklyn Atlantics.

1884- 1900

1884: The Brooklyn Atlantics join the American Association for their first professional season.

1889: Brooklyn wins its first pennant.

1890: Brooklyn transfers to the National League. Nicknamed the "Bridegrooms", as a result of seven players getting married around the same time in 1888, the team won the championship with an 86-23 record.

1890: The term "Trolley Dodgers" was attached to the Brooklyn ballclub because of the complex maze of trolley cars that weaved through the borough of Brooklyn. The name was then shortened to just "Dodgers" starting in 1911.

1897: Baltimore manager Ned Hanlon joins Brooklyn and brings with him several of Baltimore's top stars, including "Wee" Willie Keeler, Hughie Jennings, Joe Kelley, Jim Hughes and Doc McJames.

1899: More Oriole players, including Joe "Iron Man" McGinnity, come to Brooklyn after Baltimore is dropped when the National League cuts back from 12 teams to eight.

1901- 1920

1909: The career of leftfielder Zach Wheat begins. In 18 years with Brooklyn, Wheat would bat .317 and eventually play in more games (2.322) than any other Dodger.

1912: Owner Charles Ebbets sells 50 percent of the team to Ed and Steve McKeever for $100,000 to obtain the funding needed to finish construction of Ebbets Field. Ebbets broke ground on his field on March 4.

1913: The Dodgers play an exhibition game on April 5 in the unofficial opening of the field. On April 9, the Dodgers dedicate 18,000-seat Ebbets Field in a game against the Phillies.

1914: The beginning of the managerial era of Wilbert Robinson, who would manage Brooklyn through 1931.

1916: The club plays in its first World Series, with a young Babe Ruth pitching for the opposing and series winning Boston Red Sox. Ruth would join the Dodgers as a first-base coach in the late 1930s, the last time the Bambino would wear a major league uniform.

1918: Pitcher Burleigh Grimes breaks in with the Dodgers and goes 19-9 with a 2.13 ERA. Grimes would win 158 games for the Dodgers over the next nine years, including four 20+ win seasons.

1920: The team wins its second league pennant, but loses the World Series to the Cleveland Indians. Brooklyn wouldn't appear in another World Series until 1941.

1921- 1940

1921 – 1939: The team finishes fifth or lower (out of eight teams) 14 of the next 18 seasons. As a result, the team is referred to as the "Daffiness Dodgers" through most of the 1930's.

1925: Co-owner Charles Ebbets dies, leaving his 50 percent ownership to his wife and children. A week later, another co-owner, Ed McKeever dies, leaving his 25 percent to his family. Wilbert Robinson is elected as president shortly after their deaths.

1930: Outfielder Babe Herman concludes the 1930 season with a .393 batting average, but amazingly finishes second behind the Giants Bill Terry, who wins the league batting title with a .401 average.

1931: The Wilbert Robinson managerial era ends, but not before Robinson wins a Brooklyn record 1,375 games in 18 seasons. Four different managers would parade through the decade after Robinson, including Max Carey (1932-33), Casey Stengel (1934-36), Burleigh Grimes (1937-38) and Leo Durocher (1939-46, 1948).

1932: Outfielder Lefty O'Doul earns the National League batting title with a .368 average.

1933: Second baseman Tony Cuccinello becomes the first Dodger ever to be selected to an All-Star Game

1938: Larry MacPhail is hired as the team's executive vice president to rebuild the Dodgers from near bankruptcy.

1939: MacPhail hires Cincinnati's broadcaster Red Barber, effectively ending an agreement among the three New York clubs prohibiting radio broadcasts.

1939: Dodgers play the first televised baseball game, against Cincinnati, on August 26.

1941- 1960

1941: The Dodgers return to the World Series for the first time since 1920, only to lose in five games to the New York Yankees. The team would win National League pennants in 1947, 1949, 1952, and 1953, but lose the World Series to the Yankees in all of them before finally knocking off the Bronx Bombers in 1955.

1942: McPhail resigns as team president to enter the army and is replaced by Branch Rickey. The team hires Walter O'Malley as its lawyer.

1945: Rickey, O'Malley and John Smith buy 50 percent of the team from Ebbets heirs for $750,000 to obtain 75 percent control of the team.

1947: An historical first on April 11 as Brooklyn breaks baseball's color line with the signing of Jackie Robinson. Four days later, Robinson becomes the first black player to play in a major league baseball game.

1947: On April 17, another Dodger legend begins his Hall-of-Fame career: Duke Snider.

1948: The Dodgers begin their long association with Vero Beach, Florida as their spring training home.

1950: O'Malley takes control of the Dodgers on October 26 from the Rickey and Smith family.

1950: Broadcaster Vin Scully begins his long association with the Dodgers.

1953: Walter Alston is named manager. Alston manages a Dodger record 23 seasons and claims four World Series championships.

1955: On June 4, Sandy Koufax makes his Dodger debut.

1955: The Dodgers win their first World Series championship, defeating the New York Yankees in seven games on October 4.

1956: Pitcher Don Newcombe makes baseball history when he becomes the first player to win both the Cy Young and MVP awards in the same season.

1957: After New York officials deny O'Malley's request to build a more modern stadium in Brooklyn on a specific piece of land, the Dodger owner announces on October 8 that the team would move to Los Angeles after 68 seasons in Brooklyn. In an attempt to bring baseball to all parts of the country, the Giants also announce that they would move to San Francisco the same year.

1958: On January 28, catcher Roy Campanella's car hits a pole and overturns after skidding on a patch of ice, breaking his neck and paralyzing him, thus ending his 10-year baseball career at age 35.

1958: On April 15, the Dodgers play their first game after moving to Los Angeles, losing 8-0 to the Giants in San Francisco.

1958: On April 18, the Dodgers play their first home game in Los Angeles, beating San Francisco 6-5 before 78,762 fans.

1959: The Dodgers win their first World Series championship in Los Angeles, defeating the Chicago White Sox in six games on October 8.

1961- 1980

1962: Pitcher Don Drysdale wins the Cy Young Award; speedster Maury Wills wins league the MVP after stealing 104 bases; Tommy Davis wins the batting crown and posts a club record 153 RBI; and pitcher Sandy Koufax leads the league in ERA.

1963: Dodger Stadium opens on April 10.

1963: Dodgers win the World Series, defeating the New York Yankees in four games while limiting the Yankees to just four runs.

1965: Dodgers win their second World Series in three years, defeating the Minnesota Twins in seven games on October 14.

1966: Sandy Koufax abruptly retires after the Dodger's World Series loss to the Baltimore Orioles because of arm issues. The 30 year-old Koufax tallied a 27-9 record with a 1.73 ERA that season.

1970: Peter O'Malley is appointed Dodgers president.

1973: The infield foursome of Steve Garvey, Dave Lopes, Bill Russell and Ron Cey play the first of eight straight seasons together.

1974: Dodgers earn their first World Series trip in eight years, losing to the Oakland Athletics in five games.

1976: Manager Walter Alston retires after 23 years. Tommy Lasorda takes over for Alston and proceeds to win National League pennants in his first two seasons, becoming only the second National League manager to achieve that feat.

1977: The Dodgers make history when four members of the team hit 30 or more home runs in one season: Steve Garvey (33), Reggie Smith (32), Ron Cey (30) and Dusty Baker (30).

1980: Dodger Stadium plays host to its first All-Star game.

1981- 2000

1981: On Opening Day, rookie Fernando Valenzuela starts for an injured Jerry Reuss and blanks the Houston Astros, 2-0, at Dodger Stadium, beginning "Fernandomania."

1981: Dodgers win the World Series, defeating the New York Yankees in six games.

1982: Dave Lopes is traded to the Oakland Athletics for Lance Hudson on February 8, and fan favorite Steve Garvey signs as a Free Agent with the San Diego Padres on December 21.

1983: Ron Cey is traded to the Chicago Cubs for Dan Cataline and Vance Lovelace on January 19, leaving only Bill Russell in an infield that had been intact since 1973.

1988: The Dodgers win the World Series, defeating the Oakland Athletics in five games, sparked by Kirk Gibson's game one heroics.

1990: The Dodgers celebrate their 100th anniversary in the National League.

1992: The Dodgers complete their worst season in franchise history with a 63-99 record.

1996: Tommy Lasorda retires as manager for health reasons after 20 seasons. Bench coach Bill Russell replaces him.

1997: Peter O'Malley announces his family will sell Dodgers franchise on January 6.

1998: Baseball owners overwhelmingly approve the sale of the Los Angeles Dodgers from Peter O'Malley to Rupert Murdoch's Fox Group on March 19 for $350 million.

1999: The Dodgers celebrate 50 years in Los Angeles.

2001- 2020

2001: Shawn Green belts a Dodger-record 49 home runs while also setting Los Angeles club marks for extra-base hits (84) and total bases (358).

2002: Dan Evans takes over as General Manager.

2002: Eric Gagne sets a club mark with 52 saves.

2004: Major League Baseball unanimously approves the sale of the Dodgers to Frank McCourt, opening up a new chapter in the history of the Dodgers. Paul DePodesta is named general manager, replacing Dan Evans.

2004: The Dodgers win 93 games and capture their first National League West Division title since 1995. The team sets a club record with 53 come-from-behind wins.

2008: Joe Torre becomes manager.

2010: After a fourth place finish, Joe Torre steps down as manager and is replaced by Don Mattingly.

2013: Club wins 15 consecutive road games, becoming the first National League team to do that since 1957.

2016: Vin Scully's final season at the microphone.

2017: The Dodgers play and lose their first of two straight World Series, falling in seven games to the Houston Astros in 2017, and in five games to the Boston Red Sox in 2018.

2018: The Dodgers win 90-plus games for the sixth consecutive season, a feat only previously accomplished once in franchise history, 1951-56.

2019: The Dodgers win a franchise-record 106 games and their seventh consecutive National League West crown, but fail to make it to the World Series for the third straight year.

2019: The Dodgers belt a National League record 279 home runs, fourth most in Major League history.

2019: Dodger players club a Major League record eight home runs on opening day.

2020: The Dodgers win their seventh World Series, beating the Tampa Bay Rays in six games in a season shortened due to the Covid-19 pandemic.

Book Sources

- *"Baseball Almanac"*: https://www.baseball-almanac.com/
- *"Baseball Reference"*: https://www.baseball-reference.com/
- *"Retro Sheet"*: https://www.retrosheet.org
- *"Society for American Baseball Research"*: https://sabr.org/
- *"MLB.com"*: https://www.mlb.com/dodgers/history
- *Las Vegas Sun:*
  https://lasvegassun.com/news/1998/mar/21/dodgers-timeline-important-dates-in-dodgers-histor/

Author's Bio

Jeff Wagner is a native of the Bay Area in California, and has been a fan of Major League Baseball for over 50 years.

Jeff is a fan of all Bay Area sport teams, including the San Jose Sharks and Golden State Warriors, as well as teams from both the San Francisco and Oakland sides of the bay: San Francisco 49ers/Giants and the Oakland Raiders/A's, making him a dying breed as this is almost unheard of today in the Bay Area! Jeff has written several blogs on his experiences:

- Our Bay Area teams have been very good to us: http://drummerjeff.blogspot.com/2012/10/our-bay-area-sport-teams-have-been-very.html
- My Top 10 Favorite Moments in Bay Area Sports History: https://drummerjeff.blogspot.com/2019/04/my-top-10-favorite-moments-in-bay-area.html
- My Top 10 Toughest Moments in Bay Area Sports History: https://drummerjeff.blogspot.com/2019/04/my-top-10-toughest-moments-in-bay-area.html

Jeff also likes playing the drums, and enjoys a blessed life with his wife Amy and their Pug Celia.

Other Books Written by Jeff:

They Played Baseball for the Giants? (*ISBN-10: 1481931865 / ISBN-13: 978-1481931861*)

They Played Baseball for the Yankees? (*ISBN-10: 161170295X / ISBN-13: 978-1611702958*)

Pug Shots: The Many Faces of a Chinese Pug (*ISBN-10: 1481931865 / ISBN-13: 978-1481931861*)

.